T0153776

Cohen's Cornucopia
to Twist the Tongue and Jerk the Jaw

COHEN'S CORNUCOPIA

TO TWIST THE TONGUE AND JERK THE JAW

collected by Mark Cohen
illustrated by Colin West

Patrick Hardy Books

Patrick Hardy Books
28 Percy Street
London W1P 9FF

First published in 1983

ISBN 0 7444 0001 5

Printed in Great Britain by
St Edmundsbury Press
Bury St Edmunds, Suffolk

Photoset by Rowland Phototypesetting Limited
Bury St Edmunds, Suffolk

Contents

Permissions

Peculiar People

Timothy Titus took two ties
To tie two tups to two tall trees,
To terrify the terrible Thomas a Tullamees.
How many Ts in *that*?

Cinderella dressed in yella
Went downstairs to meet her fella,
On the way her panties busted –
How many people were disgusted?

Chickety choo, choo, choo, cha,
Knockaby nooby knockaby da,
Oddawy dusty canty coo,
Ollipy follipy china moo,
In China once there lived a man,
His name was Tiddy-ran-tan.
His legs were long, his feet were small –
This Chinaman couldn't walk at all.

The Drunken Sailor

Amidst the mists and coldest frosts,
With barest wrists and stoutest boasts,
He thrusts his fists against the posts,
And still insists he sees the ghosts.

The Modern Major-General

I am the very model of a modern Major-General,
I've information vegetable, animal and mineral;
I know the kings of England, and I quote the fights historical,
From Marathon to Waterloo, in order categorical;
I'm very well acquainted, too, with matters mathematical,
I understand equations, both the simple and quadratical,

About binomial theorem I'm teeming with a lot o' news –
With many cheerful facts about the square of the
    hypotenuse,
I'm very good at integral and differential calculus,
I know the scientific names of beings animalculous;
In short, in matters vegetable, animal, and mineral,
I am the very model of a modern Major-General.

W. S. Gilbert

Old, oily Ollie oils oily autos.

Tim,
the
thin
twin
tinsmith.

Theophilus Thistledown, the successful thistle sifter,
In sifting a sieve of unsifted thistles,
Thrust three thousand thistles
Through the thick of his thumb.
If, then, Theophilus Thistledown, the successful thistle
    sifter,
In sifting a sieve full of unsifted thistles,
Thrust three thousand thistles
Through the thick of his thumb,
See that thou, in sifting a sieve of unsifted thistles,
Do not get the unsifted thistles stuck in *thy* tongue.

Swim son, swim, show me you're a swimmer,
Swim just how the swans swim – you know how the swans swim.
Six sharp sharks are come to swipe your limb,
So swim as swiftly as you can, and swim son, swim.

Sister Susie's sewing shirts for soldiers.
Such saucy, soft, short shirts our shy young sister Susie
    sews;
Some soldiers send epistles, say they'd sooner sleep on
    thistles
Than the saucy, soft, short shirts our shy young sister Susie
    sews.

Arctic architects constructed artistic Etruscan arches.

Peg-leg Reg dredged the sludge grudgingly.

Herbert likes Hubert
And Hubert likes Schubert.
And Schubert liked sherbet
Like Hubert likes Herbert.

Colin West

A thatcher of Thatchwood went to Thatchet a-thatching;
Did a thatcher of Thatchwood go to Thatchet a-thatching?
If a thatcher of Thatchwood went to Thatchet a-thatching,
Where's the thatching the thatcher of Thatchwood has
thatched?

Three crooked cripples went through Cripplegate,
And through Cripplegate went three crooked cripples.

Moses supposes his toeses are roses;
But Moses supposes erroneously:
For nobody's toeses are posies of roses
As Moses supposes his toeses to be.

I know a man called Michael Finnegan --
He grew whiskers on his chinnegan.
Along came a wind and blew them in again;
Poor old Michael Finnegan,
Begin again.

Robert Rowley rolled a round roll round;
A round roll Robert Rowley rolled round;
Where rolled the round roll Robert Rowley rolled round?

Round and round the rugged rock
The ragged rascal ran.
How many Rs are there in *that*?
Now tell me if you can?

Bertha and Gertie

Can you translate this one?

Boita and Goitie sat on de coib
Reading de Woild and de Joinal.
Said Boita to Goitie, 'Der's a woim in de doit.'
Said Goitie to Boita, 'De woim don't hoit,
But it soitenly looks infoinal!'

My Sister Sybil

Sipping soup, my sister Sybil
Seems inclined to drool and dribble.
If it wasn't for this foible,
Meal-times would be more enjoyable!

Colin West

Three Ghostesses

Three little ghostesses
Sitting on postesses,
Eating buttered toastesses,
Greasing their fistesses,
Up to their wristesses.
Oh, what beastesses
To make such feastesses!

Out for the
Count
and
Needles and Pins

Een-a, deen-a,
Dine-a, dust,
Cat-ll-a, ween-a,
Wine-a, wust,
Spit, spot, must be done,
Twiddlum, twaddlum, twenty-one.
O-U-T, spells out,
A nasty, dirty dishclout.

Eeny, pheeny, figgery, fegg,
Deely, dyly, ham and egg.
Calico back, and stony rock,
Arlum barlum, bash!

Zeenty, peenty, heathery, mithery,
Bumfy, leery, over, Dover,
Saw the King of Heazle Peazle
Jumping o'er Jerusalem Dyke:
Black fish, white trout,
Eerie, ourie, you're out.

A man and a woman begat
Bouncing triplets named Nat, Pat and Tat.
It was fun in the breeding
But hell in the feeding –
There was not a spare tit for Tat.

The
sixth
sheik's
sixth
sheep's
sick.

Say in one breath:

My father he left me, just as he was able,
One bowl, one bottle, one table,
Two bowls, two bottles, two tables,
Three bowls, three bottles, three tables,
Four bowls, four bottles, four tables,
Five bowls, five bottles, five tables,
Six bowls, six bottles, six tables.

I need not your needles,
They're needless to me.
For needing needles is
Needless, you see.
But did my neat trousers
But need to be kneed,
I then should have need
Of your needles indeed.

Hell's Bells

Skvallerbytta, bing, bång,
Går i alla gårdar,
Slickar alla skålar.

Tail teller, bing, bang,
Pops into every snicket,
To lick up every slop.

Does your shirt-shop
stock short socks with spots?

When a twister a-twisting will twist him a twist,
For the twisting of his twist, he three twines doth entwist;
But if one of the twines of the twist do untwist,
The twine that untwisteth, untwisteth the twist.

Untwirling the twine that untwisteth between,
He twirls, with his twister, the two in a twine;
Then twice having twisted the twines of the twine,
He twitcheth, the twice he had twined, in twain.

The twain that, in twining, before in the twine
As twines were entwisted; he now doth untwine;
'Twixt the twain inter-twisting a twine more between,
He, twirling his twister, makes a twist of the twine.

An old scold sold a cold coal shovel.

A canner exceedingly canny,
One morning remarked to his granny,
'A canner can can
Anything that he can,
But a canner can't can a can, can he?'

Sixty needles and sixty pins,
Sixty dirty Republikins.

Sixty rats and sixty cats,
And sixty dirty Democrats.

Counting sheep in the Pennines from one to ten . . .
Yan . . . Tyan . . . Tethera . . . Methera . . . Pimp . . .
Sethera . . . Lethera . . . Hovera . . . Dovera . . . Dick

Awful
Animals

My dame hath a lame tame crane,
My dame hath a crane that is lame.
Pray, gentle Jane, let my dame's tame crane
Feed and come home again.

Okere gb'okere g'ope
is not
Hickory Dickory Dock
in Yoruba, but means:
The squirrel climbed a palm tree with another
squirrel on its back.

Can you imagine an imaginary menagerie manager
imagining managing an imaginary menagerie?

The Gaping, Wide-mouthed, Waddling Frog

A gaping, wide-mouthed, waddling frog.

TWO pudding ends that won't choke a dog,
Nor a gaping, wide-mouthed, waddling frog.

THREE monkeys tied to a log,
Two pudding ends that won't choke a dog,
Nor a gaping, wide-mouthed, waddling frog.

FOUR horses stuck in a bog,
Three monkeys tied to a log,
Two pudding ends that won't choke a dog,
Nor a gaping, wide-mouthed, waddling frog.

FIVE puppies by our dog Ball,
That daily for their breakfast call;
Four horses stuck in a bog,
Three monkeys tied to a log,
Two pudding ends that won't choke a dog,
Nor a gaping, wide-mouthed, waddling frog.

SIX beetles against the wall,
Close to an old woman's apple stall;

Five puppies by our dog Ball,
That daily for their breakfast call;
Four horses stuck in a bog,
Three monkeys tied to a log,
Two pudding ends that won't choke a dog,
Nor a gaping, wide-mouthed, waddling frog.

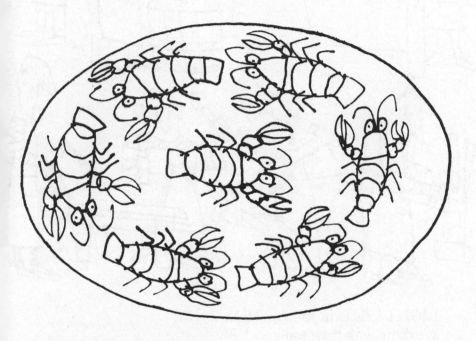

SEVEN lobsters in a dish,
As good as any heart can wish;
Six beetles against the wall,
Close to an old woman's apple stall;
Five puppies by our dog Ball,
That daily for their breakfast call;
Four horses stuck in a bog,
Three monkeys tied to a log,
Two pudding ends that won't choke a dog,
Nor a gaping, wide-mouthed, waddling frog.

EIGHT joiners in Joiners' Hall,
Working with their tools and all;
Seven lobsters in a dish,
As good as any heart can wish;
Six beetles against the wall,
Close to an old woman's apple stall;
Five puppies by our dog Ball,
That daily for their breakfast call;
Four horses stuck in a bog,
Three monkeys tied to a log,
Two pudding ends that won't choke a dog,
Nor a gaping, wide-mouthed, waddling frog.

NINE peacocks in the air,
I wonder how they all got there,
You don't know, nor I don't care;
Eight joiners in Joiners' Hall,
Working with their tools and all;
Seven lobsters in a dish,
As good as any heart can wish;
Six beetles against the wall,
Close to an old woman's apple stall;
Five puppies by our dog Ball,
Who daily for their breakfast call;
Four horses stuck in a bog,
Three monkeys tied to a log,
Two pudding ends that won't choke a dog,
Nor a gaping, wide-mouthed, waddling frog.

TEN comets in the sky,
Some low and some high;
Nine peacocks in the air,
I wonder how they all got there,
You don't know, nor I don't care;
Eight joiners in Joiners' Hall,
Working with their tools and all;
Seven lobsters in a dish,
As good as any heart can wish;
Six beetles against the wall,
Close to an old woman's apple stall;
Five puppies by our dog Ball,
Who daily for their breakfast call;
Four horses stuck in a bog,
Three monkeys tied to a log,
Two pudding ends that won't choke a dog,
Nor a gaping, wide-mouthed, waddling frog.

ELEVEN ships sailing on the main,
Some bound for France, and some for Spain,
I wish them all safe back again;
Ten comets in the sky,
Some low and some high;
Nine peacocks in the air,
I wonder how they all got there,
You don't know, and I don't care;
Eight joiners in Joiners' Hall,
Working with their tools and all;
Seven lobsters in a dish,
As good as any heart can wish;
Six beetles against the wall,
Close to an old woman's apple stall;
Five puppies by our dog Ball,
Who daily for their breakfast call;
Four horses stuck in a bog,
Three monkeys tied to a log,
Two pudding ends that won't choke a dog,
Nor a gaping, wide-mouthed, waddling frog.

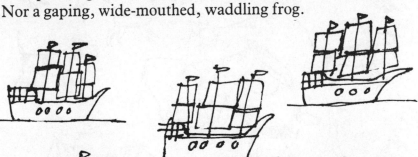

TWELVE huntsmen with horns and hounds,
Hunting over other men's grounds;
Eleven ships sailing on the main,
Some bound for France, and some for Spain,
I wish them all safe back again;
Ten comets in the sky,
Some low and some high;
Nine peacocks in the air,
I wonder how they all got there,
You don't know, and I don't care;
Eight joiners in Joiners' Hall,
Working with their tools and all;
Seven lobsters in a dish,
As good as any heart can wish;
Six beetles against a wall,
Close to an old woman's apple stall;
Five puppies by our dog Ball,
Who daily for their breakfast call;
Four horses stuck in a bog,
Three monkeys tied to a log,
Two pudding ends that won't choke a dog,
Nor a gaping, wide-mouthed, waddling frog.

Polly Cox's ox ate hollyhocks.
Now the hollyhocks-eating ox
Lies in a great mahogany box.

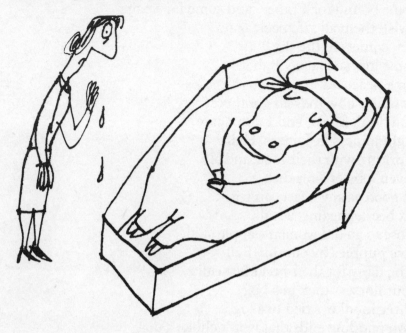

If a woodchuck could chuck wood,
How much wood would a woodchuck chuck,
If a woodchuck could chuck wood?
He would chuck, he would, as much as he could,
If a woodchuck could chuck wood.

Six Sicilian snakes sibilantly sang six silly serenades
to six Serbian serpents.

The cat ran over the roof with a lump of raw liver.

Fuzzy Wuzzy was a bear,
Fuzzy Wuzzy had no hair.
Fuzzy Wuzzy wasn't fuzzy,
Was he?

A tricky tongue-twister in an African click language, Xhosa:
Iqaqa laziqikaqika kwaze kwaqhawka uqhoqhoqha.
Which of course means:
The skunk rolled down and ruptured his larynx,
Which of course means:
The skunk sunk and caught his throat.

If a dog chews shoes what shoes would he choose to chew?
Too few for sure. You're a choosier shoe-chewer.

Shrewd Simon's Short Stories

The Sniffle

In spite of her sniffle
Isabel's chiffle.
Some girls with a sniffle
Would be weepy and tiffle;
They would look awful,
Like a rained-on waffle,
But Isabel's chiffle
In spite of her sniffle.
Her nose is more red
With a cold in her head,
But then, to be sure,
Her eyes are bluer.
Some girls with a snuffle,
Their tempers are uffle.
But when Isabel's snivelly
She's snivelly civilly,
And when she's snuffly
She's perfectly luffly.

Ogden Nash

My grandmother sent me a new-fashioned three-cornered
  cambric country-cut handkerchief,
Not an old-fashioned three-cornered cambric country-cut
  handkerchief,
But a new-fashioned three-cornered cambric country-cut
  handkerchief.

Polly, Dolly, Kate and Molly

Polly, Dolly, Kate and Molly,
All are filled with pride and folly.
Polly tattles,
Dolly wriggles,
Katy rattles,
Molly giggles.
Whoever knew such constant rattling,
Wriggling, giggling, noise and tattling?

To Marie

When the breeze from the bluebottle's blustering blim
Twirls the toads in a tooroomaloo,
And the whiskery whine of the wheedlesome whim
Drowns the roll of the rattatattoo,
Then I dream in the shade of the shally-go-shee,
And the voice of the bally-molay
Brings the smell of stale poppy-cods blummered in blee
From the willy-wad over the way.

Ah, the shuddering shoo and the blinketty-blanks
When the yungalung falls from the bough
In the blast of a hurricane's hicketty-hanks
On the hills of the hocketty-how!
Give the rigmarole to the clangery-whang,
If they care for such fiddlededee;
But the thingumbob kiss of the whangery-bang
Keeps the higgledy-piggle for me.

L'Envoi
It is pilly-po-doddle and aligobung
When the lollipop covers the ground,
Yet the poldiddle perishes punketty-pung
When the heart jimmy-coggles around.
If the soul cannot snoop at the giggle-some cart,
Seeking surcease in gluggety-glug,
It is useless to say to the pulsating heart,
'Panky-doodle ker-chuggetty-chug!'

This is fiendishly and Finnishly mean:
Itseksesikö itkeskelet,
Yksikseksikö yskiskelet?
Are you moaning to yourself, are you coughing on your own?

Esau Wood sawed wood.

Esau Wood would saw wood. Oh, the wood that Wood would saw! One day Esau Wood saw a saw saw wood as no other wood-saw Wood ever saw would saw wood.

Of *all* the wood-saws Wood ever saw saw wood, Wood never saw a saw that would saw like the wood-saw Wood saw would.

Now Esau saws with that saw he saw saw wood.

Once upon a barren moor,
There dwelt a bear, also a boar.
The bear could not bear the boar,
The boar thought the bear a bore.
At last the bear could bear no more
The boar that bored him on the moor.
And so one morn he bored the boar –
The boar will bore the bear no more.

Many an anemone sees an enemy anemone.

Algy met a bear,
The bear met Algy,
The bear was bulgy –
The bulge was Algy.

Shrewd Simon Short

Shrewd Simon Short sewed shoes. Seventeen summers saw Simon's small, shabby shop still standing, saw Simon's selfsame squeaking sign still swinging swiftly, specifying:

Simon's spouse, Sally Short, sewed sheets, stitched shirts, stuffed sofas.

Simon's stout sturdy sons – Stephen, Samuel, Saul, Silas – sold sundries. Stephen sold silks, satins, shawls. Samuel sold saddles, stirrups. Saul sold silver spoons, specialities. Silas sold Sally Short's stuffed sofas.

Simon's second son, Samuel, saw Sophia Sophronia Spriggs somewhere. Sweet, sensible, smart Sophia Sophronia Spriggs. Sam soon showed strange symptoms.

Surprisingly, Sam sighed sorrowfully, sang several serenades slyly, sought Sophia Spriggs' society, seldom stood selling saddles.

Simon stormed, scowled severely, said, 'Sam seems so silly singing such senseless songs.'

'Softly,' said sweet Sally. 'Sam's smitten. Sam's spied some sweetheart.'

'Smitten!' snarled Simon. 'Scatterbrained simpleton! Sentimental, silly schoolboy!'

Sally sighed sadly. Summoning Sam, she spoke sympathizingly. 'Sam,' said she, 'Sire seems singularly snappish. So, Sonny, stop strolling streets so soberly, stop singing sly serenades. Sell saddles sensibly, Sam. See Sophia Sophronia Spriggs speedily.'

'So soon?' said Sam, startled.

'So soon, surely,' said Sally, smilingly, 'specially since Sire shows such spirit.'

So Sam, somewhat scared, sauntered slowly storewards, shaking stupendously. 'Sophia Sophronia Spriggs . . . Sam Short's spouse . . . sounds splendid,' said Sam softly.

Sam soon spied Sophia starching shirts, singing softly. Seeing Sam, she stopped, saluting Sam smilingly.

Sam stuttered shockingly. 'Sp-sp-splendid s-s-summer s-s-season, So-So-Sophia.'

'Somewhat sultry,' suggested Sophia.

'S-s-sartin,' said Sam.

'Still selling saddles, Sam?' said Sophia.

'S-s-sartin,' said Sam.

Silence, seventeen seconds.

'Sire shot sixteen snipe Saturday, Sam,' said Sophia.

Silence, seventy-seven seconds.

'See sister Sue's sunflowers,' said Sophia socially, stopping such stiff silence.

Such sprightly sauciness stimulated Sam strangely. So, swiftly speaking, Sam said, 'Sue's sunflowers seem saying, "Sophia Sophronia Spriggs, Samuel Short stroll serenely, seek some sparkling streams, sing some sweet, soul-stirring strain. . . ."'

Sophia snickered, so Sam stopped. She stood silently several seconds.

Said Sam, 'Stop smiling, Sophia. Sam's seeking some sweet spouse!'

She still stood silently.

'Speak, Sophia, speak! Such silence speculates sorrow.'

'Seek Sire Spriggs, Sam,' said Sophia.

Sam sought Sire Spriggs.

Sire Spriggs said, 'Sartin.'

There was a man and his name was Dob,
And he had a wife, and her name was Mob,
And he had a dog, and he called it Cob,
And she had a cat called Chitterabob.
'Cob,' says Dob,
'Chitterabob,' says Mob.
Cob was Dob's dog,
Chitterabob Mob's cat.

Trentatre trentini venivano da Trento,
tutti e trentatre trottando
Which means something slightly different from:
Twenty-three Trentines travelled from Trent,
Twenty-three travelled in ten trains.

The sweetest girl I ever saw
Sat sipping cider through a straw.

Shrewd
Simon's
Stumbling
Stories

The Leith police dismisseth us,
I'm thankful, sir, to say;
The Leith police dismisseth us,
They thought we sought to stay.
The Leith police dismisseth us,
We both sighed sighs apiece,
And the sigh that we sighed as we said goodbye
Was the size of the Leith police.

John Ball's Gun

John Ball shot them all.

John Scott made the shot,
  But John Ball shot them all.

John Brammer made the rammer,
John Scott made the shot,
  But John Ball shot them all.

John Wyming made the priming,
And John Brammer made the rammer,
And John Scott made the shot,
  But John Ball shot them all.

John Block made the stock,
And John Wyming made the priming,
And John Brammer made the rammer,
And John Scott made the shot,
  But John Ball shot them all.

John Crowder made the powder,
And John Block made the stock,
And John Wyming made the priming,
And John Brammer made the rammer,
And John Scott made the shot,
  But John Ball shot them all.

John Puzzle made the muzzle,
And John Crowder made the powder,
And John Block made the stock,
And John Wyming made the priming,
And John Brammer made the rammer,
And John Scott made the shot,
  But John Ball shot them all.

John Clint made the flint,
And John Puzzle made the muzzle,
And John Crowder made the powder,
And John Block made the stock,
And John Wyming made the priming,
And John Brammer made the rammer,
And John Scott made the shot,
  But John Ball shot them all.

John Patch made the match,
John Clint made the flint,
John Puzzle made the muzzle,
John Crowder made the powder,
John Block made the stock,
John Wyming made the priming,
John Brammer made the rammer,
John Scott made the shot,
  But John Ball shot them all.

Betty Botter bought some butter,
But, she said, the butter's bitter;
If I put it in my batter
It will make my batter bitter,
But a bit of better butter,
That would make my batter better.
So she bought a bit of butter
Better than her bitter butter,
And she put it in her batter
And the batter was not bitter.
So 'twas better Betty Botter
Bought a bit of better butter.

Nelly Dean is fiendishly mean,
To jump on Lucy's juicy jelly beans.

The Rake's Progress

Born lorn,
Dad bad,
Nurse worse;
'Drat brat!'
School – fool,
Work shirk,
Gal pal,
Splash cash,
Bets – debts,
Pop shop.
Nil – till!
Boss – loss,
Wired 'Fired!'
Scrub pub,
Drink – brink –
Found drowned.
'De se';*
Grief brief.

C. W. Brodribb

*'Did it himself'

Le ver vert va vers le verre vert.
The green grub goes to the green glass.

You can take a tub with a rub and a scrub in a two-foot tank
  of tin,
You can stand and look at the whirling brook and think
  about jumping in,
You can chatter and shake in the cold black lake, but the
  kind of bath for me
Is to take a dip from the side of a ship, in the trough of the
  rolling sea.

W. S. Gilbert

The Kangaroo

A kangaroo sat on an oak,
To my inkum-kiddy-kum ki-mo,
Watching a tailor mend his coat,
To my inkum-kiddy-kum ki-mo.

   Chorus:
   Ki-mi-nee-ro, kiddy-kum keer-o,
   Ki-mi-nee-ro ki-mo,
   Ba-ba-ba-ba billy-illy-inkum,
   Inkum-kiddy-kum ki-mo.

Bring me my arrow and my bow,
To my inkum-kiddy-kum ki-mo,
Till I go shoot that kangaroo,
To my inkum-kiddy-kum ki-mo.

The old man fired, he missed his mark,
To my inkum-kiddy-kum ki-mo,
He shot the old sow through the heart,
To my inkum-kiddy-kum ki-mo.

Bring me some 'lasses* in a spoon,
To my inkum-kiddy-kum ki-mo,
Till I go heal that old sow's wound,
To my inkum-kiddy-kum ki-mo.

O now the old sow's dead and gone,
To my inkum-kiddy-kum ki-mo,
Her little ones go waddling on,
To my inkum-kiddy-kum ki-mo.

*molasses

It was a stormy night
on Christmas day
as they fell awake
on the Santa Fe

Turkey, jelly
and the ship's old cook
all jumped out
of a recipe book

The jelly wobbled
the turkey gobbled
and after them both
the old cook hobbled

Gobbler gobbled
Hobbler's Wobbler
Hobbler gobbled
Wobbler's Gobbler.

Gobbly-gobbler
gobbled Wobbly
Hobbly-hobbler
Gobbled Gobbly.

Gobble gobbled
Hobble's Wobble
Hobble gobbled
gobbled Wobble

gobble gobble
wobble wobble
hobble gobble
wobble gobble

Michael Rosen

The Modern Hiawatha

He killed the noble Mudjokivis.
Of the skin he made him mittens,
Made them with the fur side inside,
Made them with the skin side outside.
He to get the warm side inside,
Put the inside skin side outside;
He to get the cold side outside,
Put the warm side fur side inside.
That's why he put the fur side inside,
Why he put the skin side outside,
Why he turned them inside outside.

Fish,
Flies and
Feathers

Once an ant
Met a bat.
Said the bat
To the cat,
'Why the dog
Don't the elephant
Get the fish out of here?'

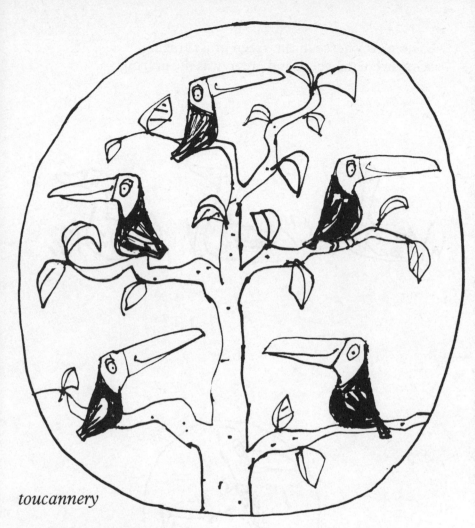

toucannery

whatever one toucan can do
is sooner done by toucans two
and three toucans it's very true
can do much more than two can do

and toucans numbering two plus two can
manage more than all the zoo can
in fact there is no toucan who can
do what four or three or two can

Jack Prelutsky

Three grey geese in the green grass grazing,
Grey were the geese and green was the grazing.

Addle-pated Albert Ross
Ate a hapless albatross.
'Twould have been a happier happening
Had the addle-pated albatross
Eaten hapless Albert Ross.

Each sixth chick sat on a stick.

A selfish shellfish smelt a stale fish.
If the stale fish was a smelt
Then the selfish shellfish smelt a smelt.

Swan swam over the sea,
Swim, swan, swim!
Swan swam back again,
Well swum, swan!

Did Kitty wake
The kittiwake,
Or did the kittiwake
Wake Kitty?

Colin West

The third bird heard the shepherd's absurd words.

A fly and a flea flew up in a flue.
Said the fly to the flea, 'What shall we do?'
'Let's fly,' said the flea.
'Let's flee,' said the fly.
So they fluttered and flew up a flaw in the flue.

Alaba la labalaba l'abara

Which means:
Alaba took a swipe at a butterfly.

Here's one for speedy Swedish sailors:
sju sjösjuka sjöjungfrur.
Which means:
Seven seasick mermaids.

A blue-backed blackbird blew big bubbles.

Did you ever ever ever
In your life, did you ever
See a whale catch a snail by the tail?
No, I never never never
In my life, no I never
Saw a whale catch a snail by the tail.

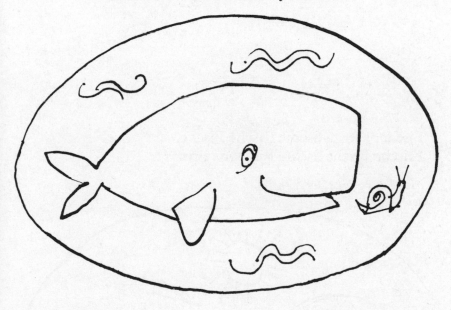

A pleasant place to place a plaice is a place where a plaice is pleased to be placed.

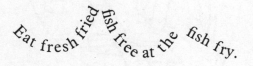

Eat fresh fried fish free at the fish fry.

Un pécheur pêchait sous un pêcher,
le pêher empêhait le pêcheur de pêcher.
Which is French for:
A sinner fished beneath a peach tree.
The peach tree prevented the sinner fishing.

Fischer's Fritz fischte frische Fische.
Frische Fische fischte Fischer's Fritz.

Fritz Fischer fishes for fresh fish.

Just Follow the Instructions and You Can't Go Wrong

Oh, such silliness!
Silly willy-nilliness,
Dopey hillybilliness,
Rolling down the hilliness!

Oh, such craziness!
First of April Dayziness,
Giddy, goopy gayziness,
Bumpy dumb horseplayziness!

Oh, such sappiness!
Ridiculous slaphappiness,
Throw away his cappiness,
Jump into his lappiness!

Oh, such hilarity!
Falling down the stairity,
Tipping over chairity,
Shaving off your hairity!

Ghostliness and ghoulishness!
Push him in the poolishness,
Staying home from schoolishness—
Oh, such foolishness!

William Cole

Busy Day

Pop in
pop out
pop over the road
pop out for a walk
pop in for a talk
pop down to the shop
can't stop
got to pop

got to pop?

pop where?
pop what?

well
I've got to
pop round
pop up
pop into town
pop out and see
pop in for tea

pop down to the shop
can't stop
got to pop

got to pop?

pop where?
pop what?

well
I've got to
pop in
pop out
pop over the road
pop out for a walk
pop in for a talk . . .

Michael Rosen

Did you eever iver ever in your leaf life loaf
See the deevil divil devil kiss his weef wife woaf?
No, I neever niver never in my leaf life loaf
Saw the deevil divil devil kiss his weef wife woaf.

Shave a cedar shingle-thin.

Tie a knapsack strap over three shy thrushes.

Sink Song

Scouring out the porridge pot,
Round and round and round!

Out with all the scraith and scoopery,
Lift the eely ooly droopery,
Chase the glubbery slubbery gloopery
Round and round and round!

Out with all the doleful dithery,
Ladle out the slimy slithery,
Hunt and catch the hithery thithery,
Round and round and round!

Out with all the obbly gubbly,
On the stove it burns so bubbly.
Use the spoon and use it doubly,
Round and round and round!

J. A. Lindon

Yellow Butter

Yellow butter purple jelly red jam black bread

Spread it thick
Say it quick

Yellow butter purple jelly red jam black bread

Spread it thicker
Say it quicker

Yellow butter purple jelly red jam black bread

Now repeat it
While you eat it

Yellow butter purple jelly red jam black bread

Don't talk
With your mouth full!

Mary Ann Hoberman

King's Orders

I mean that at present you can't marry a peasant, even though the peasant is pleasant. If you marry a pleasant peasant at present I shall not have you in my presence. You mustn't marry a peasant at present or you leave my presence.

Interesting Italian information:

Sotto la panca
La capra campa;
Sopra la panca
La capra crepa.

or:

Beneath the bench
A goat may graze;
Above the bench
The goat will croak.

The
Computer's
First
Christmas
Card

jollymerry
hollyberry
jollyberry
merryholly
happyjolly
jollyjelly
jellybelly
bellymerry
hollyheppy
jollyMolly
marryJerry
merryHarry
hoppyBarry
heppyJarry
bobbyheppy
berryjorry
jorryjolly
moppyjelly
Mollymerry
Jerryjolly
bellyboppy
jorryhoppy
hollymoppy
Barrymerry
Jarryhappy
happyboppy
bobbyjolly
jollymerry
merrymerry
merrymerry
merryChris
ammerryasa
Chrismerry
asMERRYCHR
YSANTHEMUM

Edwin Morgan

It's not the hunting on Hampstead Heath that hurts the horse's hooves, but the hammer, hammer, hammer on the hard high-road.

Un chasseur ne sachant pas chasser sans son chien est un mauvais chasseur.
*A hunter unable to hunt without his hound
is hardly an able hunter.*

Crazy and Hazy Places

New York's unique,

unique New York.

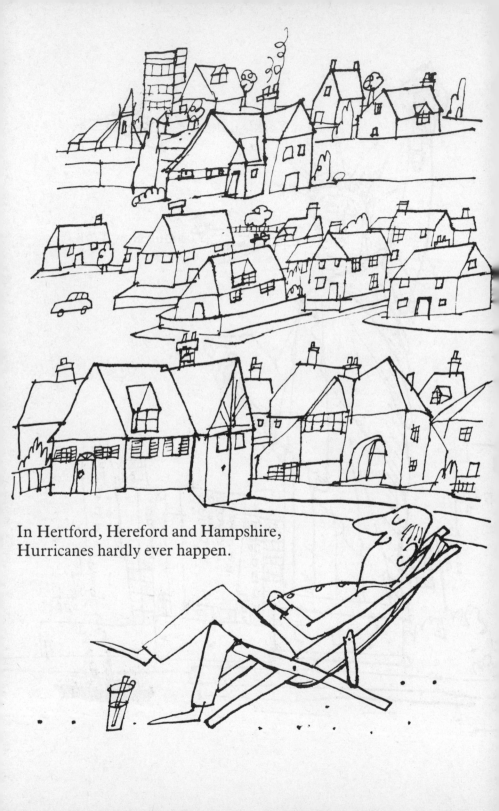

In Hertford, Hereford and Hampshire,
Hurricanes hardly ever happen.

The rain in Spain
falls mainly
in the plain.

The Cars in Caracas

The cars in Caracas
create a ruckukus,
a four-wheeled fracacas,
taxaxis and truckes.

Cacaphono-comic,
the tracaffic is farcic;
its weave leads the stomach
to turn Caracarsick.

John Updike

*The Venezuelan writer and political leader
Miguel Otero Silva returned this courtesy to
his city with a translation into Spanish:*

Los Carros en Caracas

Los carros en Caracas
sufren de patatuses;
chillan sus matracas
taxaxis y busbuses.

Cacófono-estrambótico
el tráfico es traumático;
y te estruja el estómago
su oleaje caracásico.

A Yoruba gob-stopper:

Koto kotoko po l'ona Kotopo,

Which means: There are too many pot-holes on the way to Kotopo.

Peter
Piper's
Practical
Principles of
Plain and
Perfect
Pronunciation

Read this through saying it aloud and see how fast you can do it.
Time yourself and add on 10 seconds for each mistake.

Andrew Airpump asked his aunt her ailment;
Did Andrew Airpump ask his aunt her ailment?
If Andrew Airpump asked his aunt her ailment,
Where was the ailment of Andrew Airpump's aunt?

Billy Button bought a buttered biscuit;
Did Billy Button buy a buttered biscuit?
If Billy Button bought a buttered biscuit,
Where's the buttered biscuit Billy Button bought?

Captain Crackskull cracked a Catchpoll's Cockscomb;
Did Captain Crackskull crack a Catchpoll's Cockscomb?
If Captain Crackskull cracked a Catchpoll's Cockscomb
Where's the Catchpoll's Cockscomb Captain Crackskull cracked?

Davy Dolldrum dreamed he drove a dragon;
Did Davy Dolldrum dream he drove a dragon?
If Davy Dolldrum dreamed he drove a dragon,
Where's the dragon Davy Dolldrum dreamed he drove?

Enoch Elkrig ate an empty eggshell;
Did Enoch Elkrig eat an empty eggshell?
If Enoch Elkrig ate an empty eggshell,
Where's the empty eggshell Enoch Elkrig ate?

Francis Fribble figured on a Frenchman's filly;
Did Francis Fribble figure on a Frenchman's filly?
If Francis Fribble figured on a Frenchman's filly,
Where's the Frenchman's filly Francis Fribble figured on?

Gaffer Gilpin got a goose and gander;
Did Gaffer Gilpin get a goose and gander?
If Gaffer Gilpin got a goose and gander,
Where's the goose and gander Gaffer Gilpin got?

Humphrey Hunchback had a hundred hedgehogs;
Did Humphrey Hunchback have a hundred hedgehogs?
If Humphrey Hunchback had a hundred hedgehogs,
Where are the hundred hedgehogs Humphrey Hunchback had?

Inigo Impey itched for an Indian image;
Did Inigo Impey itch for an Indian image?
If Inigo Impey itched for an Indian image,
Where's the Indian image Inigo Impey itched for?

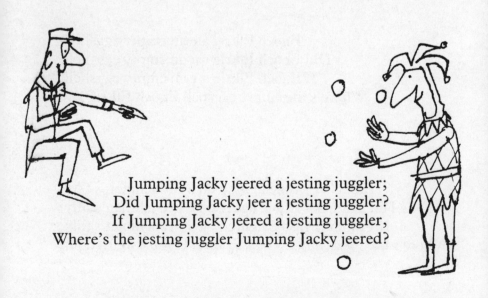

Jumping Jacky jeered a jesting juggler;
Did Jumping Jacky jeer a jesting juggler?
If Jumping Jacky jeered a jesting juggler,
Where's the jesting juggler Jumping Jacky jeered?

Kimbo Kemble kicked his kinsman's kettle;
Did Kimbo Kemble kick his kinsman's kettle?
If Kimbo Kemble kicked his kinsman's kettle,
Where's the kinsman's kettle Kimbo Kemble kicked?

Lanky Lawrence lost his lass and lobster;
Did Lanky Lawrence lose his lass and lobster?
If Lanky Lawrence lost his lass and lobster,
Where are the lass and lobster Lanky Lawrence lost?

Matthew Mendlegs missed a mangled monkey;
Did Matthew Mendlegs miss a mangled monkey?
If Matthew Mendlegs missed a mangled monkey,
Where's the mangled monkey Matthew Mendlegs missed?

Neddy Noodle nipped his neighbour's nutmegs;
Did Neddy Noodle nip his neighbour's nutmegs?
If Neddy Noodle nipped his neighbour's nutmegs,
Where are the neighbour's nutmegs Neddy Noodle nipped?

Oliver Oglethorpe ogled an owl and oyster;
Did Oliver Oglethorpe ogle an owl and oyster?
If Oliver Oglethorpe ogled an owl and oyster,
Where are the owl and oyster Oliver Oglethorpe ogled?

Peter Piper picked a peck of pickled pepper;
Did Peter Piper pick a peck of pickled pepper?
If Peter Piper picked a peck of pickled pepper,
Where's the peck of pickled pepper Peter Piper picked?

Quixote Quicksight quizzed a queerish quidbox;
Did Quixote Quicksight quiz a queerish quidbox?
If Quixote Quicksight quizzed a queerish quidbox,
Where's the queerish quidbox Quixote Quicksight quizzed?

Rory Rumpus rode a raw-boned racer;
Did Rory Rumpus ride a raw-boned racer?
If Rory Rumpus rode a raw-boned racer,
Where's the raw-boned racer Rory Rumpus rode?

Sammy Smellie smelt a smell of smallcoal;
Did Sammy Smellie smell a smell of smallcoal?
If Sammy Smellie smelt a smell of smallcoal,
Where's the smell of smallcoal Sammy Smellie smelt?

Tip-Toe Tommy turned a Turk for twopence;
Did Tip-Toe Tommy turn a Turk for twopence?
If Tip-Toe Tommy turned a Turk for twopence,
Where's the Turk for twopence Tip-Toe Tommy turned?

Uncle's usher urged an ugly urchin;
Did Uncle's usher urge an ugly urchin?
If Uncle's usher urged an ugly urchin,
Where's the ugly urchin Uncle's usher urged?

Villiam Veedon viped his vig and vaistcoat;
Did Villiam Veedon vipe his vig and vaistcoat?
If Villiam Veedon viped his vig and vaistcoat,
Where are the vig and vaistcoat Villiam Veedon viped?

Walter Waddle won a walking wager;
Did Walter Waddle win a walking wager?
If Walter Waddle won a walking wager,
Where's the walking wager Walter Waddle won?

X Y Z have made my brains to crack-o,
X smokes, Y snuffs, and Z chews tobacco;
Yet oft by X Y Z much learning's taught;
But Peter Piper beats them all to nought.